Living or Nonliving?

by Kelli Hicks

Science Content Editor:
Kristi Lew

Educational Media

rourkeeducationalmedia.com

Scan for Related Titles and Teacher Resources

Science content editor: Kristi Lew
A former high school teacher with a background in biochemistry and more than 10 years of experience in cytogenetic laboratories, Kristi Lew specializes in taking complex scientific information and making it fun and interesting for scientists and non-scientists alike. She is the author of more than 20 science books for children and teachers.

www.rourkeeducationalmedia.com

Photo credits: Cover © Awei, Adi, Cover logo frog © Eric Pohl, test tube © Sergey Lazarev; Page 5 © olena2552; Page 6 © Anat-oli; Page 7 © Igorsky; Page 9 © Rudchenko Liliia; Page 11 © Darren Hubley; Page 12 © Monkey Business Images; Page 13 © oksana2010; Page 14 © Volodymyr Krasyuk; Page 15 © Anyka; Page 16 © Sharon Morris; Page 17 © steamroller_blues; Page 18 © DavidEwingPhotography; Page 19 © patpitchaya; Page 20 © Arch-Man; Page 21 © Olga Popova, Maksym Bondarchuk, Africa Studio, Wolfe Larry, fivespots, Eric isselée

Editor: Jeanne Sturm

Cover and page design by Nicola Stratford, bdpublishing.com

Library of Congress Cataloging-in-Publication Data

Hicks, Kelli L.
 Living or nonliving? / Kelli Hicks.
   p. cm. -- (My science library)
Includes bibliographical references and index.
ISBN 978-1-61741-743-6 (Hard cover) (alk. paper)
ISBN 978-1-61741-945-4 (Soft cover)
1. Life (Biology)--Juvenile literature. I. Title.
QH501.H53 2012
570--dc22
                            2011003872

Also Available as:

Rourke Educational Media
Printed in the United States of America,
North Mankato, Minnesota

rourkeeducationalmedia.com
customerservice@rourkeeducationalmedia.com • PO Box 643328 Vero Beach, Florida 32964

Table of Contents

It's Alive

Think about the world around you. How do you know if something is alive? If it needs food, water, and air to survive, it is a living thing.

Goats breathe in the fresh air as they look for a stream to get a drink of water.

What's for Dinner?

Living things need food to make **energy.** A pig eats slop. It must be living.

A farmer mixes cornmeal and water to make slop used to feed pigs and other livestock.

7

Plants are living, too. They make their own food with a little help from the Sun.

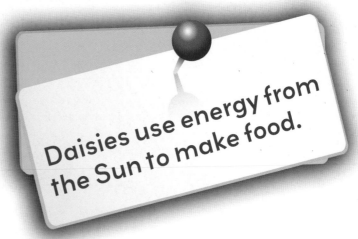

Daisies use energy from the Sun to make food.

Do you feed a **computer**? If it doesn't need food to survive, it is nonliving.

Does It Need Air?

Take a deep **breath**. People are living things and need air to breathe.

Does a rock breathe? It must be nonliving.

Are You Thirsty?

If it is a living thing, it needs water. Water helps living things stay **healthy**.

A horse drinks water. It must be living.

A bicycle doesn't drink water.
It must be nonliving.

Does It Move?

Living things can move. Some living things hop, skip, or run. Plants move, too. They turn to face the Sun, and they open their flowers to **bloom.**

Sunflowers bend or turn towards the Sun to catch the most sunlight.

A book cannot move on its own.
It must be nonliving.

Can you pick which things are living and which ones are nonliving?

SHOW What You Know

1. Can you name two things that are alive?

2. Is a toy robot living? How do you know?

3. How do you know if something is living or nonliving?

Glossary

bloom (BLOOM): when a plant's flowers appear

breath (BRETH): the air that you take into your lungs and out again

computer (kuhm-PYOO-tur): an electronic machine that can store and retrieve large amounts of information

energy (EN-ur-jee): the ability to do work and be active without getting tired

healthy (HEL-thee): being fit and well

Index

Websites

www.rbnc.org/schoolunits/natpyra.htm

www.fi.edu/tfi/units/life

www.firstschoolyears.com/science/index.htm

About the Author

Kelli Hicks tries to show she is living by playing sports, walking the dog, eating healthy food, and drinking lots of water. She lives in Tampa, Florida, with her husband, her children Mackenzie and Barrett, and their dog Gingerbread.

Meet The Author!
www.meetREMauthors.com

24